Ramen Noodle
RECIPES

Publications International, Ltd.

Pictured on the front cover (clockwise from top left): Chicken Nuggets with Spicy Tomato Dipping Sauce *(page 10)*, Ramen "Spaghetti" Tacos *(page 116)*, Open-Faced "S'Mores" *(page 134)*, and Cheesy Italian Noodle Bake *(page 56)*.

Pictured on the back cover: Stuffed Bell Peppers *(page 60)*.

ISBN-13: 978-1-4508-4948-7
ISBN-10: 1-4508-4948-2

Library of Congress Control Number: 2012931034

Manufactured in China.

8 7 6 5 4 3 2 1

Microwave Cooking: Microwave ovens vary in wattage. Use the cooking times as guidelines and check for doneness before adding more time.

Preparation/Cooking Times: Preparation times are based on the approximate amount of time required to assemble the recipe before cooking, baking, chilling or serving. These times include preparation steps such as measuring, chopping and mixing. The fact that some preparations and cooking can be done simultaneously is taken into account. Preparation of optional ingredients and serving suggestions is not included.

Contents

Simple Starters

Timesaving Thai Wraps

1	package (3 ounces) chicken-flavored ramen noodles*
2	teaspoons creamy peanut butter
1½	cups packaged coleslaw mix
½	cup diced cooked chicken
2	(6-inch) flour tortillas
	Soy sauce (optional)

Discard seasoning packet.

1 Cook noodles according to package directions; do not drain. Add peanut butter, one teaspoon at a time, stirring until melted. Stir in coleslaw mix and chicken; cover and set aside 2 minutes.

2 Spoon noodle mixture onto tortillas. Sprinkle with soy sauce, if desired. Wrap and serve immediately.

Tip: These small wraps make a great appetizer or light snack.

Western Ramen Frittata

1 package (3 ounces) chicken-flavored ramen noodles, broken into chunks

8 eggs

1 cup shelled edamame, thawed if frozen

6 ounces ham steak, cut into ½-inch cubes

4 green onions, thinly sliced

2 teaspoons vegetable oil

6 ounces fresh mozzarella cheese, cut into ½-inch cubes

1 Preheat broiler.

2 Cook noodles according to package directions. Drain and rinse with cold water.

3 Whisk eggs and 1 teaspoon of the seasoning packet in large bowl. Discard remaining seasoning packet. Stir in edamame, ham, green onions and noodles.

4 Heat oil in 12-inch broiler-proof skillet over medium heat. Add egg mixture; stir gently to form large curds. Top with mozzarella cheese. Cover; cook 6 minutes or until edge of eggs are set. Run rubber spatula along side occasionally to prevent sticking.

5 Uncover skillet; transfer to broiler. Broil 6 minutes or until frittata is puffed and set. Let stand 5 minutes. Slide onto serving plate or cutting board; cut into wedges.

7-Layer Dip

1	package (3 ounces) ramen noodles, any flavor, crushed*
2	tablespoons dried taco seasoning mix
3	ripe avocados, diced
1	jalapeño pepper, finely chopped**
2	tablespoons finely chopped cilantro
2	tablespoons lime juice
1	clove garlic, minced
½	teaspoon salt
1	can (about 15 ounces) refried beans
1	container (16 ounces) sour cream
2	cups shredded Mexican Cheddar-Jack cheese
2	medium tomatoes, diced
3	green onions, thinly sliced
	Tortilla chips

*Discard seasoning packet.

**Jalapeño peppers can sting and irritate the skin, so wear rubber gloves when handling peppers and do not touch your eyes.

1 Combine noodles with taco seasoning mix in medium bowl; mix well.

2 Mash avocados, jalapeño, cilantro, lime juice, garlic and salt in large bowl.

3 Spread refried beans in bottom of 8-inch glass baking dish. Layer sour cream, noodles, avocado mixture, cheese, tomatoes and green onions evenly over beans. Serve immediately or cover and refrigerate for up to 8 hours. Serve with tortilla chips.

Chicken Nuggets with Spicy Tomato Dipping Sauce

Makes 4 servings

Spicy Tomato Dipping Sauce (recipe follows)

½	cup panko bread crumbs
½	cup grated Parmesan cheese
1	package (3 ounces) ramen noodles, any flavor, finely crushed*
1	teaspoon garlic powder
1	teaspoon dried basil
½	teaspoon salt
¼	teaspoon black pepper
1	egg, lightly beaten
1½	pounds boneless skinless chicken breasts, cut into 1×2½-inch strips
½	cup vegetable oil

Discard seasoning packet.

1 Prepare Spicy Tomato Dipping Sauce; set aside. Combine panko, cheese, crushed noodles, garlic powder, basil, salt and pepper in large bowl. Place egg in shallow dish. Dip chicken in egg; shake off excess. Coat with crumb mixture.

2 Heat oil in large skillet over medium heat. Cook chicken in batches about 5 minutes or until cooked through, turning once. Serve with Spicy Tomato Dipping Sauce.

Spicy Tomato Dipping Sauce

Makes 1½ cups sauce

1	tablespoon olive oil
1	small onion, chopped
2	cloves garlic, minced
¼	teaspoon ground red pepper
1	can (about 14 ounces) fire-roasted diced tomatoes

1 Heat oil in medium skillet. Add onion and garlic; cook and stir about 3 minutes or until onion is tender and golden brown. Stir in red pepper.

2 Remove skillet from heat; add tomatoes. Process in blender or food processor until smooth. Return to skillet and cook about 10 minutes or until thickened and reduced to 1½ cups.

Simple Starters

Coconut Shrimp

Makes 4 servings

Spicy Orange-Mustard Sauce (recipe follows)

¾	cup all-purpose flour
¾	cup beer or water
1	egg
¾	teaspoon baking powder
½	teaspoon salt
¼	teaspoon ground red pepper
1	cup flaked coconut
2	packages (3 ounces each) ramen noodles, any flavor, crushed*
20	jumbo raw shrimp, peeled and deveined
2	cups vegetable oil

Discard seasoning packets.

1 Prepare Spicy Orange-Mustard Sauce; set aside.

2 Whisk flour, beer, egg, baking powder, salt and red pepper in medium bowl. Combine coconut and noodles in another medium bowl. Dip shrimp in beer batter; shake off excess. Coat with coconut mixture.

3 Heat oil in large skillet to 350°F. Cook shrimp in batches 3 minutes or just until golden, turning once halfway through cooking. Drain on paper towel-lined plate. Serve with Spicy Orange-Mustard Sauce.

Spicy Orange-Mustard Sauce: Combine ¼ cup coarse grain or Dijon mustard, 2 tablespoons honey, 2 tablespoons orange juice, 2 teaspoons orange peel, ½ teaspoon ground red pepper and ¼ teaspoon ground ginger in small bowl until blended.

Tip: Use one hand to dip the shrimp in the beer batter and the other hand to coat with coconut mixture. This way, your hands will not mix up the mixtures and create a larger mess.

Crispy Ramen Noodle Pancake

1 large (8-inch) pancake or 2 servings

2 packages (3 ounces each)
   chicken-flavored ramen noodles*

2 green onions, thinly sliced

2 tablespoons water

2 teaspoons oyster sauce

1 teaspoon cornstarch

⅛ teaspoon black pepper

3 tablespoons vegetable oil, divided

3 ounces shiitake mushrooms, stems removed, sliced

2 medium heads bok choy, cut into ¼-inch-wide strips

Reserve one seasoning packet, discard the other seasoning packet.

1 Cook noodles according to package directions. Drain and rinse with cold water. Transfer to large bowl. Toss with green onions and seasoning packet.

2 Combine water, oyster sauce, cornstarch and pepper in small bowl.

3 Heat 1 tablespoon oil in large skillet over medium-high heat. Add noodle mixture to skillet; press down evenly with spatula to form a pancake. Cook 5 to 7 minutes or until bottom is crisp and golden brown. Slide onto serving plate; add 1 tablespoon oil to skillet. Invert pancake into skillet and cook 5 minutes until crisp and golden brown. Return pancake to plate and keep warm.

4 Heat remaining 1 tablespoon oil in skillet. Add mushrooms; cook 2 minutes or until tender, stirring occasionally. Add bok choy; cook 2 minutes or until stems are crisp-tender. Add sauce mixture and cook 30 seconds or until vegetables are glazed, stirring frequently. Spoon vegetables over pancake.

Simple Starters

Noodlicious
Salads & Sides

Oriental Ramen Salad

2	tablespoons butter or margarine
1	package (3 ounces) dry oriental-flavor ramen noodle soup, noodles crumbled and seasoning packet reserved
½	cup sliced almonds
⅔	cup (5-fluid-ounce can) NESTLÉ® CARNATION® Evaporated Fat Free Milk
⅔	cup vegetable oil
3	tablespoons white vinegar
2	tablespoons granulated sugar
2	packages (10 ounces each) romaine-radicchio salad greens
4	green onions, sliced diagonally

MELT butter in large skillet. Add crumbled ramen noodles and nuts; cook, stirring constantly, until noodles are golden. Remove from pan; cool.

PLACE evaporated milk, oil, ramen seasoning packet, vinegar and sugar in blender; cover. Blend until smooth.

COMBINE salad greens, noodle mixture, green onions and dressing in large bowl; toss to coat well. Serve immediately.

Green Bean Mushroom Casserole

Makes 6 servings

1	pound fresh green beans, ends trimmed
4	tablespoons vegetable oil, divided
4	shallots, thinly sliced
8	ounces cremini mushrooms, quartered
1	can (10¾ ounces) condensed cream of mushroom soup
½	cup milk
¼	teaspoon freshly ground black pepper
1	package (3 ounces) ramen noodles, any flavor, broken into small pieces*
⅛	teaspoon salt

Discard seasoning packet.

1 Preheat oven to 350°F. Bring water to a boil in large saucepan over high heat. Add green beans and cook 4 minutes. Drain and rinse with cold water.

2 Heat 3 tablespoons oil in large skillet over medium heat. Add shallots; cook 10 minutes or until softened and golden brown. Drain on paper towels. Heat remaining 1 tablespoon oil in skillet over medium-high heat. Add mushrooms; cook 7 minutes or until browned.

3 Combine soup, milk and pepper in large bowl. Add beans and mushrooms. Spoon into ungreased 1½-quart casserole; bake 20 minutes. Increase oven temperature to 400°F. Combine shallots, noodles and salt; sprinkle over casserole. Bake 5 minutes.

Noodlicious Salads & Sides

Southwestern Salad

Makes 4 to 6 servings

2	hearts of romaine lettuce, cut crosswise into ½-inch-thick strips
1	cup frozen corn, thawed
1	cup halved cherry tomatoes
8	ounces boneless skinless chicken breasts, cooked and diced
1	ripe avocado, diced
1	red bell pepper, diced
1	can (about 15 ounces) black beans, rinsed and drained

Dressing

1½	tablespoons minced shallot
¼	cup lime juice
2	teaspoons honey
⅓	cup olive oil
½	teaspoon kosher salt
¼	teaspoon black pepper
2	tablespoons finely chopped fresh cilantro (optional)

1	package (3 ounces) ramen noodles, any flavor, broken into small pieces*

Discard seasoning packet.

1 Combine romaine, corn, tomatoes, chicken, avocado, bell pepper and black beans in large bowl; toss well.

2 Whisk shallot, lime juice, honey, oil, salt, black pepper and cilantro in medium bowl. Add to salad mixture; toss to coat. Sprinkle with noodles.

Oriental Crab & Noodle Salad

Makes 4 servings

1 package (10 ounces) Chinese curly noodles or
    10 ounces vermicelli

1 package (8 ounces) flaked imitation crabmeat

6 ounces (1½ cups) fresh snow peas or sugar snap peas

⅓ cup soy sauce

2 tablespoons seasoned rice vinegar

2 tablespoons dark sesame oil

1 teaspoon minced fresh ginger

½ teaspoon minced garlic

¼ teaspoon red pepper flakes

1 red bell pepper, cut into strips

¼ cup thinly sliced green onions (optional)

1 Bring 3 quarts water to a boil in covered large saucepan over high heat. Add noodles; return to a boil. Cook 2 minutes. Add crabmeat and snow peas; cook 1 minute or until noodles are al dente.

2 Meanwhile, for dressing, combine soy sauce, vinegar, sesame oil, ginger, garlic and pepper flakes in large bowl; mix well.

3 Drain noodle mixture. Add noodle mixture and bell pepper to dressing; toss to coat. Arrange mixture on salad plates; sprinkle with green onions, if desired.

Asian Shrimp & Noodle Salad

Makes 6 servings

- ⅓ cup plus 2 tablespoons vegetable oil, divided
- ¼ cup cider vinegar
- 2 tablespoons FRENCH'S® Worcestershire Sauce
- 2 tablespoons light soy sauce
- 2 tablespoons honey
- 1 teaspoon grated fresh ginger or ¼ teaspoon ground ginger
- 2 packages (3 ounces each) chicken-flavor ramen noodle soup
- 1 pound shrimp, cleaned and deveined with tails left on
- 2 cups vegetables such as broccoli, carrots and snow peas, cut into bite-size pieces
- 1⅓ cups FRENCH'S® French Fried Onions, divided

1 Combine ⅓ cup oil, vinegar, Worcestershire, soy sauce, honey and ginger until well blended; set aside. Prepare ramen noodles according to package directions for soup; drain and rinse noodles. Place in large serving bowl.

2 Stir-fry shrimp in 1 tablespoon oil in large skillet over medium-high heat, stirring constantly, until shrimp turn pink. Remove shrimp to bowl with noodles. Stir-fry vegetables in remaining oil in skillet over medium-high heat, stirring constantly, until vegetables are crisp-tender.

3 Add vegetable mixture, dressing and 1 cup French Fried Onions to bowl with noodles; toss to coat well. Serve immediately topped with remaining ⅓ cup onions.

Tip: Purchase cut-up vegetables from the salad bar of your local supermarket to save prep time.

Creamy and Crunchy Coleslaw

1	tablespoon vegetable oil
2	packages (3 ounces) ramen noodles, any flavor*
½	cup sliced almonds
½	cup mayonnaise
¼	cup rice wine vinegar
2	teaspoons honey
1	teaspoon sesame oil
1	teaspoon soy sauce
	Hot pepper sauce, to taste
2	cups shredded napa cabbage
½	cup sliced green onions

Discard seasoning packets.

1 Heat vegetable oil in medium skillet over medium heat. Crush half of one package noodles into skillet; cook and stir 2 minutes. Add almonds; cook and stir 2 minutes or until golden brown. Transfer to plate.

2 Bring water to a boil in medium saucepan over medium-high heat. Add remaining noodles; cook 2 minutes. Drain and rinse with cold water.

3 Combine mayonnaise, vinegar, honey, sesame oil, soy sauce and hot pepper sauce in large bowl; mix well. Add boiled noodles, cabbage and green onions; toss to coat. Top with toasted noodles and almonds just before serving.

Broccoli Slaw

Makes 6 to 8 servings

1	package (12 ounces) broccoli slaw
6	slices bacon, crisp-cooked and crumbled
½	small red onion, chopped
1	package (3 ounces) ramen noodles, any flavor, broken into small pieces, divided*
¼	cup roasted salted sunflower seeds
1	cup reduced-fat mayonnaise
2	tablespoons sugar
2	tablespoons cider vinegar
¼	teaspoon black pepper

Discard seasoning packet.

1 Combine broccoli slaw, bacon, onion, half of noodles and sunflower seeds in large bowl.

2 Whisk mayonnaise, sugar, vinegar and pepper in small bowl. Pour over slaw mixture; stir to combine. Garnish with remaining noodles. Serve immediately.

Tip: Any chopped nuts, such as peanuts or almonds, can be substituted for the sunflower seeds.

Noodlicious Salads & Sides

Mandarin Salad

Makes 4 servings

⅓	cup olive oil
2	tablespoons cider vinegar
2	teaspoons honey
2	teaspoons dried tarragon
½	teaspoon dry mustard
¼	teaspoon salt
⅛	teaspoon ground black pepper
1	can (11 ounces) mandarin oranges, drained, and 1 tablespoon juice reserved
4	cups chopped romaine lettuce
1	package (3 ounces) ramen noodles, any flavor, lightly crushed*
½	cup toasted pecans, coarsely chopped**
¼	cup chopped red onion

Discard seasoning packet.

**To toast pecans, spread in single layer in small heavy skillet. Cook over medium heat 1 to 2 minutes or until nuts are lightly browned, stirring frequently. Remove from skillet immediately. Cool before using.*

1 Whisk oil, vinegar, honey, tarragon, mustard, salt, pepper and reserved mandarin orange juice in large bowl.

2 Add lettuce, oranges, noodles, pecans and onion to dressing; toss to combine.

Noodlicious Salads & Sides

Thai Beef Salad with Cucumber Dressing

Makes 4 servings

Cucumber Dressing (recipe follows)

1 pound extra-lean (90% lean) ground beef

½ red bell pepper, cut into thin strips

6 mushrooms, quartered

2 green onions, diagonally cut into 1-inch pieces

1 clove garlic, minced

1 tablespoon seasoned rice vinegar

1 teaspoon soy sauce

1 package (3 ounces) beef-flavored ramen noodles

Lettuce leaves

12 cherry tomatoes, halved (optional)

Mint sprigs (optional)

1 Prepare Cucumber Dressing; set aside. Brown beef in medium skillet. Drain. Add red bell pepper, mushrooms, green onions and garlic; cook until tender. Stir in vinegar, soy sauce and seasoning packet from ramen noodles.

2 Cook noodles according to package directions. Drain. Cool in bowl of ice water. Drain well before serving.

3 Arrange lettuce on four plates. Top with noodles and beef mixture. Garnish with tomatoes and mint. Serve with the dressing.

Cucumber Dressing

1 medium cucumber, coarsely chopped

½ cup coarsely chopped onion

½ cup loosely packed cilantro leaves

1 clove garlic, minced

1 tablespoon diced jalapeño or green chile pepper*

½ cup seasoned rice vinegar

Jalapeño and chili peppers can sting and irritate the skin, so wear rubber gloves when handling peppers and do not touch your eyes.

Place cucumber, onion, cilantro, garlic and jalapeño in food processor container; process 1 minute. Spoon mixture into small bowl; stir in vinegar.

Noodlicious Salads & Sides

Tuna Ramen Noodle Salad

Makes 1 serving

½   **package (3 ounces) Oriental-flavor ramen noodle soup mix**

1   **(2.6-ounce) STARKIST Flavor Fresh Pouch® Tuna (Albacore or Chunk Light)**

½   **cup julienne-strip cucumber**

½   **cup julienne-strip green or red bell pepper**

½   **cup sliced water chestnuts, cut into halves**

Dressing

2   **tablespoons rice or white vinegar**

2   **teaspoons sesame oil**

1   **teaspoon peanut butter**

⅛   **teaspoon crushed red pepper**

Cook ramen noodles according to package directions. Drain broth, reserving if desired to use as a clear soup for another meal. In a medium bowl toss noodles with tuna, cucumber, bell pepper and water chestnuts.

For Dressing, in a small shaker jar combine vinegar, oil, peanut butter and crushed red pepper. Cover and shake until well blended. Toss with noodle mixture. Serve immediately.

Mediterranean Chickpea Ramen Salad

Makes 6 to 8 servings

2   packages (3 ounces each) ramen noodles, any
      flavor, broken into small pieces*

    Juice of 1 lemon

3   tablespoons extra virgin olive oil

1   teaspoon kosher salt

½   teaspoon black pepper

1   can (about 15 ounces) chickpeas, rinsed and drained

2   tomatoes, diced

¾   cup crumbled feta cheese

½   cup diced red onion

½   English cucumber, seeded and diced

¼   cup finely chopped Italian parsley

Discard seasoning packets.

1 Cook noodles according to package directions; drain well.

2 Whisk lemon juice, oil, salt and pepper in large bowl. Add chickpeas, tomatoes, feta cheese, onion, cucumber, parsley and noodles; toss to combine.

Creamy Noodle Kugel

3	packages (3 ounces each) ramen noodles, any flavor*
¾	cup cottage cheese
¾	cup sour cream
2	eggs
⅓	cup granulated sugar
½	cup golden raisins (optional)
2	tablespoons packed brown sugar

Discard seasoning packets.

1 Preheat oven to 350°F. Spray 9-inch glass baking dish with nonstick cooking spray.

2 Bring water to a boil in large saucepan. Boil noodles 2 minutes. Drain and rinse with cold water.

3 Whisk cottage cheese, sour cream, eggs and granulated sugar in large bowl. Add noodles and raisins, if desired; toss to coat. Pour into prepared dish. Sprinkle with brown sugar.

4 Bake 35 to 40 minutes or until center is set. Serve warm or at room temperature.

Mushroom Pilaf

2   **tablespoons butter, divided**

1   **package (3 ounces) oriental-flavored ramen noodles, crumbled**

½   **cup chopped pecans**

1   **package (8 ounces) sliced mushrooms**

2   **cups hot cooked rice**

2   **tablespoons chopped fresh parsley**

1 Melt 1 tablespoon butter in large skillet over medium-high heat. Add noodles and pecans; cook and stir 3 minutes or until toasted. Remove to plate.

2 Melt remaining 1 tablespoon butter in skillet. Add mushrooms; cook and stir 8 minutes or until browned.

3 Reduce heat to medium; add rice, seasoning packet from noodles, noodle mixture and parsley; cook and stir 2 minutes or until heated through.

Tips:

If this dish will not be served right away, reserve the toasted noodles and pecans. Fold into pilaf just before serving so they stay crisp.

Add 1½ cups chopped cooked chicken to the pilaf to make a main dish.

Grilled Pork & Pineapple Ramen Salad

½   cup reduced-sodium teriyaki sauce

¼   cup FRENCH'S® Honey Mustard or FRENCH'S® Honey Dijon Mustard

2   tablespoons rice vinegar

2   tablespoons peanut oil

1   tablespoon sugar

2   packages (3 ounces each) chicken-flavored ramen noodle soup

1   pound pork tenderloin

½   fresh pineapple, cored, skinned and cut into 1-inch wedges

    Chopped green onions and red bell peppers for garnish

1 Combine teriyaki sauce, mustard, vinegar, oil and sugar in measuring cup. Prepare ramen noodles according to package directions for soup; drain and rinse noodles. Place in large serving bowl and toss with half the dressing.

2 Grill pork over medium-high heat 20 minutes or until slightly pink in center. Grill pineapple about 5 minutes just until heated through and lightly browned. Slice pork thinly and cut pineapple into chunks.

3 Arrange pork and pineapple over noodles and drizzle with remaining dressing. Garnish with green onions and red peppers if desired.

Tip: Purchase cored and skinned fresh pineapple from the produce section of the supermarket.

Greek Noodle Salad

2 packages (3 ounces each) ramen noodles, any flavor, broken in half*

3 tablespoons olive oil

Juice of 1 lemon

2 tablespoons red wine vinegar

1 teaspoon dried oregano

1 tomato, chopped

¾ cup diced cucumber

½ cup crumbled feta cheese

¼ cup chopped kalamata olives

Discard seasoning packets.

1 Bring water to a boil in medium saucepan. Boil noodles 2 minutes. Drain and rinse with cold water.

2 Combine oil, lemon juice, vinegar and oregano in large bowl. Add noodles, tomato, cucumber, feta cheese and olives; toss to coat.

Tip: This easy-to-prepare salad makes a delicious side for baked or grilled fish.

Asian Mandarin Salad

Makes 6 servings

1 package (5 to 12 ounces) DOLE® Field Greens or Chopped Romaine, or any variety salad

⅓ cup crispy noodles

⅓ cup sliced almonds, toasted

1 can (11 or 15 ounces) DOLE® Mandarin Oranges, drained

½ cup bottled Asian sesame dressing

Toss together salad blend, noodles, almonds and mandarin oranges in large serving bowl. Pour dressing over salad; toss to evenly coat. Serve.

Sunflower Salad

Makes 4 to 5 main dish servings

1	package beef ramen noodles, broken into pieces
3	cups shredded cabbage
⅓	cup chopped onion
1	large tomato, chopped
2	tablespoons bacon bits
¼	cup sunflower kernels, roasted, no salt
¼	cup shredded cheddar cheese

Boil ramen noodles for 3 to 4 minutes. Drain and rinse with cold water. Refrigerate until cool. Combine all salad ingredients in a large bowl and prepare dressing.

Dressing

¼	cup sugar
3	tablespoons sunflower oil
1½	tablespoons vinegar
1	beef seasoning packet from ramen noodles

Mix ingredients together and add to salad. Refrigerate before serving.

Favorite recipe from NATIONAL SUNFLOWER ASSOCIATION

Rio-Ramen Salad

Makes 6 servings

4	cups torn fresh spinach
4	cups broccoli slaw
6	green onions, thinly sliced (tops included)
¾	cup purchased red wine and vinegar salad dressing
½	teaspoon freshly ground black pepper
3	Texas RIO STAR® Grapefruits, 1 juiced and 2 sectioned
1	(2½ ounces) package Ramen noodles, lightly toasted and broken
¼	cup sesame seeds, lightly toasted

1 In a large bowl, toss together spinach, coleslaw mix and onions, then chill.

2 In a small jar, shake together salad dressing, pepper and ¼ cup of grapefruit juice (refrigerate remaining juice for another use), then chill.

3 Just before serving, add grapefruit sections, noodles and sesame seeds to salad.

4 Pour dressing over top and toss to evenly coat.

5 Serve immediately.

Total Time: 10 minutes

Dinner Winners

Broccoli Beef Stir-Fry

Makes 4 servings

Vegetable cooking spray
3   cups broccoli florets
1   boneless beef sirloin steak
1   can (10¾ ounces) Campbell's® Condensed Tomato Soup
¼   cup water
2   packages (2.8 ounces **each**) oriental flavor ramen noodle soup

1 Spray a 10-inch skillet with the cooking spray and heat over medium-high heat for 1 minute. Add the broccoli and stir-fry until tender-crisp. Remove the broccoli from the skillet. Remove the skillet from the heat.

2 Spray the skillet with the cooking spray and heat over medium-high heat for 1 minute. Add the beef and stir-fry until well browned. Stir in the soup, water and **1** ramen seasoning packet (reserve the remaining seasoning packet for another use) and heat to a boil. Return the broccoli to the skillet and cook until the mixture is hot and bubbling.

3 Cook the noodle soup according to the package directions without the seasoning packet. Drain the noodles well in a colander. Serve the beef mixture over the noodles.

Prep Time: 10 minutes
Cook Time: 25 minutes

Eggplant Parmesan

Makes 12 servings

2 eggs

1 teaspoon dried basil

½ teaspoon salt

¼ teaspoon black pepper

½ cup plus 2 tablespoons grated Parmesan cheese, divided

1 package (3 ounces) ramen noodles, any flavor, crushed*

¼ cup panko or other bread crumbs

2 medium eggplants (1 pound each), cut lengthwise into ¾-inch slices

2 cups vegetable oil

1 cup low-fat ricotta cheese

8 ounces shredded mozzarella cheese

1 jar (about 28 ounces) tomato sauce

Discard seasoning packet.

1 Preheat oven to 350°F. Spray 13×9-inch baking pan with nonstick cooking spray.

2 Beat eggs, basil, salt and pepper in shallow dish until blended. Combine ½ cup Parmesan cheese, crushed noodles and bread crumbs in another shallow dish. Dip eggplant in egg mixture; shake off excess. Coat both sides with crumb mixture.

3 Heat oil in large skillet. Cook eggplant in batches 4 minutes or until golden, turning once. Drain on paper towel-lined plate.

4 Combine ricotta cheese and mozzarella cheese in small bowl. Place one third of eggplant in bottom of prepared pan. Spread about 1 cup tomato sauce over eggplant. Top with half of cheese mixture; repeat layers ending with sauce. Bake 30 minutes or until eggplant is fork-tender and cheese is melted.

5 Preheat broiler. Sprinkle remaining 2 tablespoons Parmesan cheese over eggplant. Broil 6 inches from heat 3 minutes or until cheese is browned. Let stand 10 minutes before serving.

Tip: Use one hand to dip the eggplant in the egg mixture and the other hand to coat with crumbs. This way, your hands will not mix up the mixtures and create a larger mess.

Denver Quiche

1	package (3 ounces) chicken-flavored ramen noodles*
1	tablespoon vegetable oil
½	cup diced red or green bell pepper
¼	cup diced yellow onion
½	cup diced ham
6	eggs
1	cup fat-free milk
½	cup shredded Cheddar cheese
	Salt and black pepper

Discard seasoning packet.

1 Preheat oven to 375°F. Spray 9-inch pie plate with nonstick cooking spray.

2 Cook noodles according to package directions. Drain and rinse with cold water. Press noodles onto bottom of pie plate; bake 10 minutes or until lightly browned. Cool completely.

3 Heat oil in medium skillet. Add bell pepper and onion and cook 3 minutes or until crisp-tender. Add ham; cook until heated through. Spoon into crust.

4 Beat eggs and milk in medium bowl until blended. Add cheese, salt and black pepper; mix well. Carefully pour over ham mixture.

5 Bake 35 minutes or until center is puffed and knife inserted near center comes out clean. Let stand 5 minutes. Cut into wedges.

Chicken Parmesan

Makes 4 servings

½ cup all-purpose flour

1 egg, lightly beaten

1 package (3 ounces) ramen noodles, any flavor*

½ cup grated Parmesan cheese

1 teaspoon dried basil

½ teaspoon dried rosemary

½ cup shredded Italian cheese blend

4 boneless skinless chicken breasts (about 1 pound)

2 tablespoons olive oil

1 cup pasta sauce, plus additional for serving

Discard seasoning packet.

1 Preheat oven to 350°F.

2 Place flour in shallow dish. Place egg in shallow bowl. Place noodles, Parmesan cheese, basil and rosemary in food processor; process until fine crumbs are formed. Reserve ¼ cup mixture. Place remaining mixture in another shallow dish. Combine reserved noodle mixture with Italian cheese blend in medium bowl.

3 Dip chicken into flour, then egg, then noodle mixture. Place on clean plate.

4 Heat oil in large ovenproof skillet. Cook chicken 8 minutes per side or until golden brown. Top with sauce and cheese mixture. Bake 15 minutes or until no longer pink in center. Serve with additional sauce.

Teriyaki Meatloaf

Makes 4 to 6 servings

1	tablespoon vegetable oil
1	package (8 ounces) thinly sliced mushrooms
½	cup chopped green onions
1	package (3 ounces) ramen noodles, any flavor, crushed*
½	cup teriyaki sauce
1	egg, lightly beaten
1½	pounds (24 ounces) ground beef

Discard seasoning packet.

1 Preheat oven to 375°F.

2 Heat oil in medium skillet over medium-high heat. Add mushrooms; cook and stir 10 minutes. Add green onions; cook and stir 1 minute. Transfer to large bowl. Add noodles, teriyaki sauce and egg; stir well. Fold in beef.

3 Press beef mixture into 8×4-inch loaf pan. Bake 35 to 40 minutes or until cooked through (160°F). Let stand 10 minutes before slicing.

Tip: Serve leftovers on toasted bread or rolls as a meatloaf sandwich. A great brown bag lunch idea!

Easy Asian Chicken Skillet

Makes 4 to 6 servings

2	packages (3 ounces each) chicken-flavored ramen noodles
1	package (10 ounces) frozen broccoli florets, thawed
1	package (9 ounces) frozen baby carrots, thawed
1	tablespoon vegetable oil
1	pound boneless skinless chicken breasts, cut into thin strips
1	can (8 ounces) sliced water chestnuts, drained
¼	cup stir-fry sauce

1 Remove seasoning packets from noodles. Save one packet for another use.

2 Bring 4 cups water to a boil in large saucepan. Add noodles, broccoli and carrots. Cook over medium-high heat 5 minutes, stirring occasionally; drain.

3 Heat oil in large nonstick skillet over medium-high heat. Add chicken; cook and stir about 8 minutes or until browned.

4 Stir in noodle mixture, water chestnuts, stir-fry sauce and one seasoning packet; cook until heated through.

Cheesy Italian Noodle Bake

Makes 8 to 10 servings

4	packages (3 ounces each) ramen noodles, any flavor*
1	pound sweet Italian sausage, casings removed
2	teaspoons olive oil
1	cup diced onion
1	cup diced red bell pepper
1	teaspoon minced garlic
1	can (about 15 ounces) tomato sauce
½	cup thinly sliced fresh basil
2	cups shredded mozzarella cheese

Discard seasoning packets.

1 Preheat oven to 400°F. Grease 13×9-inch baking dish.

2 Cook noodles according to package directions. Drain and rinse with cold water. Transfer to large bowl.

3 Brown sausage in large skillet over medium-high heat 8 minutes or until well browned, stirring to break up meat. Drain on paper towel-lined plate. Transfer to bowl with noodles.

4 Heat oil in skillet. Add onion and bell pepper; cook and stir 6 minutes or until softened. Add garlic and cook 30 seconds. Transfer to bowl. Add tomato sauce and basil; stir until well combined.

5 Spread mixture evenly in prepared dish. Sprinkle with cheese. Bake 25 to 30 minutes or until bubbly and cheese is golden brown. Let stand 5 minutes before serving.

Lemon Herbed Tilapia

Makes 4 servings

2   tablespoons melted butter

   Grated peel and juice of 1 lemon, divided

1   package (3 ounces) ramen noodles, any flavor*

1   teaspoon dried dill weed

1   teaspoon dried basil

1   teaspoon dried parsley

4   tilapia fillets (about 4 ounces each)

Discard seasoning packet.

1 Preheat oven to 425°F. Line baking sheet with parchment paper.

2 Combine melted butter and lemon juice in shallow bowl. Combine noodles, dill, basil, parsley and lemon peel in food processor. Process until fine crumbs are formed; pour onto plate.

3 Dip tilapia into butter mixture, then press into noodle mixture. Place on prepared baking sheet.

4 Bake 12 minutes or until fish flakes when tested with fork.

Dinner Winners

Stuffed Bell Peppers

3   large red bell peppers, halved lengthwise and seeded

1   package (3 ounces) ramen noodles, any flavor, cut into fourths*

6   slices bacon, diced

1   cup finely chopped onion

1   teaspoon minced garlic

¼   teaspoon black pepper

1   can (about 15 ounces) cannellini beans, rinsed and drained

¾   cup shredded Gruyère cheese

1   tablespoon plus 1½ teaspoons finely chopped fresh parsley

Discard seasoning packet.

1 Preheat oven to 400°F. Place bell peppers, cut sides up, in 13×9-inch baking pan.

2 Cook noodles in boiling water in large saucepan over medium heat 2 minutes. Drain and rinse with cold water until cool. Transfer to large bowl.

3 Heat large nonstick skillet over medium-high heat. Add bacon; cook 6 to 7 minutes or until crisp and browned. Transfer to paper towel-lined plate with slotted spoon. Drain and discard all but 2 teaspoons drippings from skillet. Add onion to skillet; cook 5 minutes or until softened. Add garlic and black pepper; cook and stir 30 seconds. Transfer to bowl with noodles; stir in beans, cheese and bacon.

4 Stuff bean mixture evenly inside bell peppers. Bake 30 minutes or until filling is heated through and bell peppers are softened. Sprinkle evenly with parsley.

Cheesy Hamburger Ramen

Makes 4 servings

1	pound ground beef
1	cup diced red onion
1	teaspoon salt, divided
2	packages (3 ounces each) ramen noodles, any flavor*
1	tablespoon unsalted butter
1	tablespoon all-purpose flour
1¼	cups milk
¼	teaspoon black pepper
1	can (about 14 ounces) diced tomatoes, drained
1½	cups shredded sharp Cheddar cheese
¼	cup ketchup

Discard seasoning packets.

1 Heat large nonstick skillet over medium-high heat. Add beef; cook 2 minutes or just until beginning to brown. Add onion and ½ teaspoon salt; cook 8 minutes or until onion is softened. Transfer to large bowl; cover to keep warm.

2 Cook noodles according to package directions; drain well. Transfer to large bowl.

3 Add butter to skillet; melt over medium heat. Stir in flour; cook 1 minute. Slowly add milk, stirring constantly. Add pepper and remaining ½ teaspoon salt; cook 4 minutes or until mixture is thickened, stirring constantly. Remove from heat. Add tomatoes, cheese and ketchup; stir until cheese is melted. Add sauce to bowl; stir to combine. Serve immediately.

Ramen Chili

Makes 8 to 10 servings

2	teaspoons vegetable oil
2	pounds ground beef
2	red onions, diced
1	red bell pepper, diced
6	tablespoons chili powder
4	teaspoons salt
2	teaspoons ground cumin
¼	teaspoon ground red pepper
4	cans (about 14 ounces each) diced tomatoes with basil, garlic and oregano
2	cans (about 15 ounces each) kidney beans, rinsed and drained
2	cups water
1	package (3 ounces) ramen noodles, any flavor, broken*
1	tablespoon light brown sugar
	Sour cream, shredded Cheddar cheese and thinly sliced green onions (optional)

Discard seasoning packet.

1 Heat oil in Dutch oven over medium-high heat. Add beef; brown 6 to 8 minutes, stirring to break up meat. Transfer to large bowl with slotted spoon. Add onions and bell pepper to Dutch oven; cook 6 minutes or until softened. Add chili powder, salt, cumin and ground red pepper; cook and stir 1 minute.

2 Return beef to Dutch oven; stir in tomatoes, beans, water, noodles and brown sugar. Bring to a boil; reduce heat to medium-low and simmer 45 minutes to 1 hour, stirring occasionally. Top with sour cream, cheese and green onions, if desired.

Swedish "Meatball" Burgers

Makes 6 servings

3	tablespoons butter, divided
1	small onion, chopped
¼	cup milk
2	packages (3 ounces each) ramen noodles, any flavor, crushed*
1	egg
1	teaspoon salt, divided
½	teaspoon black pepper, divided
¼	teaspoon ground allspice
1½	pounds ground beef
¼	cup all-purpose flour
1	can (about 14 ounces) beef broth
½	cup whipping cream
	Hard rolls
	Cranberry sauce (optional)

Discard seasoning packets.

1 Melt 2 tablespoons butter in medium saucepan over medium heat. Add onion; cook 3 minutes or until translucent. Reduce heat to medium-low; add milk. Bring to a simmer. Add crushed noodles; remove from heat.

2 Whisk egg, ½ teaspoon salt, ¼ teaspoon pepper and allspice in large bowl. Add noodle mixture; stir to combine. Add beef; stir until well blended. Shape into 6 patties.

3 Preheat broiler. Broil burgers on rack 4 inches from heat 10 minutes until medium-rare (145°F), or desired doneness.

4 Melt remaining 1 tablespoon butter in saucepan. Add flour; cook 2 to 3 minutes or until lightly browned, whisking constantly. Gradually whisk in broth and cream. Bring to a boil; cook 2 minutes or until thickened. Stir in remaining salt and pepper.

5 Serve burgers on rolls with cream sauce and cranberry sauce, if desired.

Hoisin Barbecue Chicken Thighs

Makes 6 to 8 servings

⅔   cup hoisin sauce

⅓   cup barbecue sauce

3   tablespoons quick-cooking tapioca

1   tablespoon sugar

1   tablespoon reduced-sodium soy sauce

¼   teaspoon red pepper flakes

12   skinless bone-in chicken thighs (3½ to 4 pounds total)

1½   pounds uncooked ramen noodles or other pasta

    Sliced green onions (optional)

Slow Cooker Directions

1 Combine hoisin sauce, barbecue sauce, tapioca, sugar, soy sauce and red pepper flakes in slow cooker. Add chicken, meat side down. Cover; cook on LOW 8 to 9 hours.

2 Just before serving, cook noodles according to package directions. Serve chicken thighs over noodles. Sprinkle with green onions, if desired.

Tomato Chicken & Noodles

Makes 4 servings

Vegetable cooking spray

3   cups cut-up vegetables (broccoli florets, sliced carrots and green or red peppers)

1   pound skinless, boneless chicken breast halves, cut into strips

1   can (10¾ ounces) Campbell's® Condensed Tomato Soup

¼   cup water

2   packages (2.8 ounces **each**) chicken flavor ramen noodle soup, cooked according to package directions (without the seasoning packet)

1 Spray a 12-inch skillet with the cooking spray. Heat for 1 minute over medium heat. Add the vegetables and cook until they're tender-crisp, stirring occasionally. Remove the vegetables from the skillet and set aside.

2 Increase the heat to medium-high. Add the chicken to the skillet and cook until it's well browned and cooked through, stirring occasionally. Remove the chicken from the skillet and set aside.

3 Stir the tomato soup, water and **1** ramen seasoning packet in the skillet and heat to a boil. (Reserve the remaining seasoning packet for another use.) Return the vegetables and chicken to the skillet and heat through. Serve the chicken mixture over the noodles.

Prep Time: 15 minutes
Cook Time: 20 minutes

Paprika Pork with Spinach

Makes 4 servings

1 pound boneless pork loin or leg

3 tablespoons all-purpose flour

3 tablespoons vegetable oil

1 cup frozen pearl onions, thawed

1 tablespoon paprika

1 can (about 14 ounces) vegetable or chicken broth

8 ounces uncooked medium curly egg noodles or 2 to 3 packages ramen noodles, any flavor*

1 package (10 ounces) frozen leaf spinach, thawed and well drained

½ cup sour cream

Discard seasoning packets.

1 Trim fat from pork; discard. Cut pork into 1-inch cubes. Place flour and pork in resealable food storage bag; shake until well coated.

2 Heat wok over high heat about 1 minute or until hot. Drizzle oil into wok and heat 30 seconds. Add pork; stir-fry about 5 minutes or until well browned on all sides. Remove pork to large bowl.

3 Add onions and paprika to wok; stir-fry 1 minute. Stir in broth, noodles and pork. Cover and bring to a boil. Reduce heat to low; cook about 8 minutes or until noodles and pork are tender, stirring occasionally.

4 Stir thawed spinach into pork and noodles. Cover and cook until heated through. Add additional water if needed. Add sour cream; mix well. Transfer to serving dish.

Scallop Stir-Fry

Makes 4 servings

2   packages (3 ounces each) ramen noodles, any flavor*
1   tablespoon olive oil
1   pound asparagus, cut into 1-inch pieces
1   red bell pepper, cut into thin rings
3   green onions, chopped
1   clove garlic, minced
1   pound sea scallops, halved crosswise
2   tablespoons soy sauce
1   teaspoon hot pepper sauce
1   teaspoon sesame oil
    Juice of ½ lime

Discard seasoning packets.

1 Cook noodles in lightly salted boiling water according to package directions.

2 Meanwhile, heat olive oil in wok or large skillet over high heat. Add asparagus, bell pepper, green onions and garlic; stir-fry 2 minutes. Add scallops; stir-fry until scallops turn opaque.

3 Stir in soy sauce, hot pepper sauce, sesame oil and lime juice. Add noodles; heat through, stirring occasionally.

Tip: Substitute vermicelli for ramen noodles.

Creamy Beef Stir-Fry

Makes 4 servings

Vegetable cooking spray

3   cups cut-up fresh vegetables (broccoli florets, sliced carrots **and** green **or** red pepper strips)

1   boneless beef sirloin steak **or** beef top round steak, ¾-inch thick (about ¾ pound), cut into very thin strips

1   can (10¾ ounces) Campbell's® Condensed Cream of Mushroom Soup (Regular **or** 98% Fat Free)

¼   cup water

2   packages (3 ounces **each**) beef flavor ramen noodle soup

1 Spray a 10-inch skillet with the cooking spray and heat over medium-high heat for 1 minute. Add the vegetables and stir-fry until tender-crisp. Remove the vegetables from the skillet. Remove the skillet from the heat.

2 Spray the skillet with the cooking spray and heat over medium-high heat for 1 minute. Add the beef and stir-fry until well browned. Remove the beef from the skillet.

3 Stir the soup, water and **1** ramen seasoning packet in the skillet and heat to a boil. (Reserve the remaining seasoning packet for another use.) Return the vegetables and beef to the skillet and cook until the mixture is hot and bubbling.

4 Prepare the noodles according to the package directions without the seasoning packets. Drain the noodles well in a colander. Serve the beef mixture over the noodles.

Prep Time: 20 minutes
Cook Time: 20 minutes

Dinner Winners

Cashew Chicken Stir-Fry

2 tablespoons vegetable oil, divided

3 boneless, skinless chicken breasts (about 12 ounces), cut into ½-inch pieces

¼ cup reduced-sodium soy sauce, divided

2 cloves garlic, minced

1 teaspoon ground ginger

2 tablespoons cornstarch

3 cups broccoli florets

1 red bell pepper, seeded and diced

1½ cups chicken broth

1 tablespoon brown sugar, firmly packed

2 teaspoons sesame oil

½ cup FISHER® CHEF'S NATURALS® Dry Roasted Cashews

Cooked Asian noodles or rice (optional)

1 In wok or large skillet, heat 1 tablespoon vegetable oil over medium-high heat 1 minute until hot. Add chicken, 2 tablespoons soy sauce, garlic and ginger; stir-fry 4 to 5 minutes until chicken is no longer pink. Transfer chicken to platter; loosely cover to keep warm.

2 Combine cornstarch and remaining 2 tablespoons soy sauce; set aside. Add remaining 1 tablespoon vegetable oil to wok. Add broccoli and red bell pepper; stir-fry 3 to 4 minutes.

3 Return chicken to wok; add chicken broth, brown sugar and sesame oil. Cook 2 to 3 minutes until broth begins to bubble. Stir in cornstarch mixture; reduce heat to medium. Cook 3 to 4 minutes until sauce thickens. Stir in cashews. Serve over cooked noodles or rice, if desired.

Asian Ramen Beef with Almonds

Makes 4 servings

1   pound deli roast beef, sliced ⅛-inch thick

4   tablespoons teriyaki marinade

⅔   cup slivered almonds, toasted and divided

1   pound broccoli slaw

2   packages oriental flavor ramen noodles, broken into small pieces (reserve seasoning packets)

4   teaspoons butter or margarine

1 In large saucepan, bring 2 quarts of water to full boil.

2 Trim any visible fat from deli roast beef and cut into julienne strips. In microwave safe bowl, toss beef with teriyaki sauce and set aside.

3 Toast almonds on cookie sheet under broiler until lightly browned. Set aside 2 tablespoons to use for garnish.

4 Add broccoli slaw to boiling water and cook over high heat for 3 minutes. To broccoli, add ramen noodles and oriental seasoning packets, reserving ½ teaspoon of seasoning, and cook an additional 3 minutes. Drain in colander. Return to pan and toss with butter, reserved oriental seasoning and toasted almonds. Cover and keep warm.

5 Warm beef in microwave at 50 percent power for 3 minutes.

6 To serve, place noodle and broccoli mixture on platter leaving a well in the center of the platter for beef. Mound beef in center. Garnish with 2 tablespoons reserved almonds and optional garnish, if desired.

Optional Garnish: Break ½ package of ramen noodles into small pieces. Mix with ½ tablespoon teriyaki marinade. Sprinkle around edge of platter.

Favorite recipe from **North Dakota Beef Commission**

Dinner Winners

Cheesy Tuna & Noodles

3	packages (3 ounces **each**) chicken flavor ramen noodle soup
1	can (10¾ ounces) Campbell's® Condensed Cream of Mushroom Soup (Regular **or** 98% Fat Free)
¾	cup milk
⅛	teaspoon garlic powder
⅛	teaspoon ground black pepper
1	box (about 10 ounces) frozen mixed vegetables, thawed
1½	cups shredded mozzarella cheese
1	can (about 6 ounces) tuna, drained

1 Cook the ramen noodles according to the package directions. Pour off most of the cooking liquid.

2 Heat the soup, milk, garlic powder, pepper and vegetables in a 10-inch skillet over medium-high heat to a boil. Reduce the heat to low. Cover and cook for 5 minutes or until vegetables are tender.

3 Stir the cheese in the skillet and cook until the cheese is melted, stirring occasionally. Stir in the tuna and noodles and cook until the mixture is hot and bubbling.

Tip: To thaw vegetables, microwave on HIGH 4 minutes.

Prep Time: 10 minutes
Cook Time: 25 minutes

Noodle Bowls

Shrimp and Pepper Noodle Bowl

Makes 4 servings

- 2 packages (3 ounces each) shrimp-flavored ramen noodles
- 8 ounces frozen cooked medium shrimp or 1 package (8 ounces) frozen cooked baby shrimp
- 1 cup frozen bell pepper strips
- ¼ cup chopped green onions
- 1 tablespoon soy sauce
- ½ teaspoon hot pepper sauce
- 2 tablespoons chopped cilantro (optional)

1 Bring 4 cups water to a boil in large saucepan over high heat. Remove seasoning packets from noodles; set aside. Break up ramen noodles; add to water. Add shrimp and bell pepper; cook 3 minutes.

2 Add seasoning packets, green onions, soy sauce and hot pepper sauce; cook 1 minute. Garnish with cilantro.

Apricot Beef with Sesame Noodles

Makes 4 to 6 servings

1	beef top sirloin steak (about 1 pound)
3	tablespoons Dijon mustard
3	tablespoons soy sauce
2	packages (3 ounces each) ramen noodles, any flavor*
2	tablespoons vegetable oil
2	cups (6 ounces) snow peas
1	medium red bell pepper, cut into cubes
¾	cup apricot preserves
½	cup beef broth
3	tablespoons chopped green onions
2	tablespoons toasted sesame seeds**, divided

Discard seasoning packet.

**To toast sesame seeds, spread in dry, heavy skillet over medium heat 2 minutes or until golden, stirring frequently.*

1 Cut beef lengthwise in half, then crosswise into ¼-inch strips. Combine beef, mustard and soy sauce in medium resealable food storage bag. Seal bag. Shake to evenly distribute marinade; refrigerate 4 hours or overnight.

2 Cook noodles according to package directions. Drain.

3 Heat oil in large skillet over medium-high heat until hot. Add half of beef with marinade; stir-fry 2 minutes. Remove to bowl. Repeat with remaining beef and marinade. Return beef to skillet. Add snow peas and bell pepper; stir-fry 2 minutes. Add noodles, preserves, broth, green onions and 1 tablespoon sesame seeds. Cook 1 minute or until heated through. Top with remaining sesame seeds before serving.

80

Noodle Bowls

French Onion Soup

Makes 4 servings

4	tablespoons butter
1	package (3 ounces) ramen noodles, any flavor, broken into small pieces*
4	sweet yellow onions (about 2 pounds), thinly sliced
2	teaspoons sugar
1	teaspoon all-purpose flour
½	teaspoon salt
¼	teaspoon black pepper
1	cup white wine
2	cans (about 14 ounces each) reduced-sodium beef broth
1	8-inch loaf French bread, sliced into 8 rounds
1	cup (about 4 ounces) shredded fontina cheese

Discard seasoning packet.

1 Melt butter in large saucepan over medium heat. Add noodles; cook and stir 2 to 3 minutes or until golden. Add onions; cook 20 to 25 minutes or until golden and translucent, stirring occasionally.

2 Combine sugar, flour, salt and pepper; add to noodle mixture. Add wine. Cook 3 minutes or until wine evaporates, stirring to scrape up browned bits. Add broth; bring to a boil. Reduce heat and simmer, partially covered, 10 minutes.

3 Preheat oven to 450°F. Line baking sheet with foil. Toast bread slices 5 minutes or until lightly browned. Sprinkle toast evenly with cheese; bake 3 minutes or until melted. Divide soup into bowls; top each with 2 slices toast. Serve immediately.

Note: If you have four individual heatproof bowls, the toast can be baked directly on top of the soup.

Asian Chicken Squiggle Soup

Makes 6 to 7 servings

2 **cups water**

1 **can (about 14 ounces) low-sodium chicken broth**

1 **cup sliced carrots**

½ **cup sliced green onions**

½ **teaspoon ground ginger**

3 **packages (3 ounces each) chicken-flavored ramen noodles**

2 **cups chopped cooked chicken**

1 **cup frozen sugar snap peas**

2 **tablespoons lemon juice**

1 Heat water, broth, carrots, green onions and ginger in large saucepan over medium heat. Stir in contents of 1 seasoning packet from noodles; bring to a boil. (Discard remaining seasoning packets or reserve for another use.)

2 Break noodles in half; stir into vegetable mixture. Boil 2 minutes. Stir in chicken, snap peas and lemon juice; cook until heated through.

Shortcut Chicken Tortilla Soup

Makes 6 servings

2   cans (about 14 ounces each) reduced-sodium chicken broth

4   boneless skinless chicken breasts (about 1 pound)

2   jars (16 ounces each) corn and black bean salsa

3   tablespoons vegetable oil

1   tablespoon taco seasoning

1   package (3 ounces) ramen noodles, any flavor, broken into small pieces*

4   ounces Monterey Jack cheese, grated

Discard seasoning packet.

1 Bring broth to a simmer in large saucepan. Add chicken; cook 12 to 15 minutes or until no longer pink in center. Remove chicken from saucepan; set aside until cool enough to handle. Shred chicken with two forks.

2 Add salsa to saucepan; cook 5 minutes or until soup comes to a simmer. Return shredded chicken to saucepan; cook 5 minutes more until thoroughly heated through.

3 Combine oil and taco seasoning in small bowl. Add noodles; toss to coat. Cook and stir noodles in medium skillet over medium heat 8 to 10 minutes or until toasted. Top soup with toasted noodles and grated cheese.

Tip: Serve soup with lime wedges, chopped avocado or fresh cilantro on the side—top with your favorites!

Noodle Bowls

Asian Ramen Noodle Soup

Makes 4 servings

2	cans (about 14 ounces each) fat-free reduced-sodium chicken broth
4	ounces boneless pork loin, cut into thin strips
¾	cup thinly sliced mushrooms
½	cup firm tofu, cut into ¼-inch cubes (optional)
3	tablespoons white vinegar
3	tablespoons sherry
1	tablespoon reduced-sodium soy sauce
½	teaspoon ground red pepper
1	package (3 ounces) ramen noodles, any flavor, broken*
1	egg, beaten
¼	cup finely chopped green onions, green tops only

Discard seasoning packet.

1 Bring broth to a boil in large saucepan over high heat; add pork, mushrooms and tofu, if desired. Reduce heat to medium-low; simmer, covered, 5 minutes. Stir in vinegar, sherry, soy sauce and red pepper.

2 Return broth mixture to a boil over high heat; stir in ramen noodles. Cook, stirring occasionally, 5 to 7 minutes or until noodles are tender. Slowly stir in egg and green onions; remove from heat. Ladle soup into individual bowls.

Noodle Bowls

Szechuan Vegetable Lo Mein

Makes 4 servings

2	cans (about 14 ounces each) vegetable broth
2	teaspoons minced garlic
1	teaspoon minced fresh ginger
¼	teaspoon red pepper flakes
1	package (16 ounces) frozen vegetable medley, such as broccoli, carrots, water chestnuts and red bell peppers
1	package (5 ounces) Asian curly noodles or 5 ounces uncooked angel hair pasta, broken in half
3	tablespoons soy sauce
1	tablespoon dark sesame oil
¼	cup thinly sliced green onions

1 Combine broth, garlic, ginger and red pepper flakes in large deep skillet. Cover and bring to a boil over high heat.

2 Add vegetables and noodles to skillet; cover and return to a boil. Reduce heat to medium-low; simmer, uncovered, 5 to 6 minutes or until vegetables and noodles are tender, stirring occasionally.

3 Stir in soy sauce and sesame oil; cook 3 minutes. Stir in green onions; ladle into bowls.

Note: For a heartier, protein-packed main dish, add 1 package (about 14 ounces) extra firm tofu, drained and cut into ¾-inch pieces, to the broth mixture with the soy sauce and sesame oil.

Asian Noodle Soup Mix

Makes 1 soup mix

½ of a 3-ounce package ramen noodles, any flavor

1 teaspoon dried chives

¼ teaspoon sesame seeds

¼ teaspoon granulated garlic

⅛ teaspoon ground ginger

1 individually wrapped fortune cookie

1 Break noodles into chunks and place in small bowl. Sprinkle half of noodle seasoning packet, chives, sesame seeds, garlic and ginger over noodles. (Save remaining noodles and seasoning for another use.) Spoon mixture into small food storage bag. Seal; place in mug. Place wrapped fortune cookie in mug.

2 Decorate mug and attach gift tag with preparation instructions.

Asian Noodle Soup

Makes 1 serving

1½ cups water

1 Asian Noodle Soup Mix

½ cup fresh or frozen snow peas or sugar snap peas

1 Heat water in small saucepan over high heat until boiling. Add soup mix and peas; stir until blended.

2 Reduce heat to medium; simmer 3 minutes or until noodles are tender.

Noodle Bowls

Curried Turkey Noodle Soup

1	tablespoon olive oil
¾	pound turkey breast tenderloin, cut into bite-size pieces
5	cups water
2	packages (3 ounces each) chicken-flavored ramen noodles
1	tablespoon curry powder
⅛	teaspoon salt
1	cup sliced celery
1	medium apple, cored and chopped (1½ cups)
¼	cup dry roasted unsalted peanuts

1 Heat oil in large saucepan over medium-high heat. Add turkey; cook and stir 3 to 4 minutes or until no longer pink. Remove turkey; set aside.

2 Add water, seasoning packets from noodles, curry powder and salt to saucepan. Bring to a boil. Reduce heat; cover and simmer 5 minutes.

3 Break up noodles; gently stir noodles and celery into saucepan. Bring mixture to a boil. Reduce heat and simmer, uncovered, 5 minutes.

4 Stir in turkey and apple. Cook until heated through. Ladle into soup bowls. Sprinkle with peanuts.

Thai Noodle Soup

Makes 4 servings

1	package (3 ounces) ramen noodles, any flavor*
¾	pound chicken tenders
2	cans (about 14 ounces each) chicken broth
¼	cup shredded carrots
¼	cup frozen snow peas
2	tablespoons thinly sliced green onions
½	teaspoon minced garlic
¼	teaspoon ground ginger
3	tablespoons chopped fresh cilantro
½	lime, cut into 4 wedges

Discard seasoning packet.

1 Break noodles into pieces. Cook noodles according to package directions.

2 Cut chicken into ½-inch pieces. Combine broth and chicken in large saucepan or Dutch oven; bring to a boil over medium heat. Cook 2 minutes.

3 Add carrots, snow peas, green onions, garlic and ginger. Reduce heat to low; simmer 3 minutes. Add cooked noodles and cilantro; heat through. Serve soup with lime wedges.

Asian Chicken Noodle Soup

Makes 4 servings

3½ cups Swanson® Chicken Broth (Regular, Natural
     Goodness® **or** Certified Organic)

1 **teaspoon soy sauce**

1 **teaspoon ground ginger**

   Generous dash ground black pepper

1 **medium carrot, diagonally sliced**

1 **stalk celery, diagonally sliced**

½ **red pepper, cut into 2-inch-long strips**

2 **green onions, diagonally sliced**

1 **clove garlic, minced**

½ **cup broken-up uncooked curly Asian noodles**

1 **cup shredded cooked chicken**

1 Heat the broth, soy sauce, ginger, black pepper, carrot, celery, red pepper, green onions and garlic in a 2-quart saucepan over medium-high heat to a boil.

2 Stir the noodles and chicken in the saucepan. Reduce the heat to medium and cook for 10 minutes or until the noodles are done.

Tip: For an Interesting Twist: Use **1 cup** sliced bok choy for the celery and **2 ounces uncooked** cellophane noodles for the curly Asian noodles. Reduce the cook time to 5 minutes.

Prep Time: 5 minutes
Cook Time: 20 minutes

Noodle Bowls

Easy Chicken & Noodles

Makes 4 servings

1¼ pounds skinless, boneless chicken breasts, cut into cubes

1 can (10¾ ounces) Campbell's® Condensed Cream of Mushroom Soup (Regular **or** 98% Fat Free)

1¾ cups water

2 cups frozen vegetable combination (broccoli, cauliflower, carrots)

2 packages (2.8 ounces **each**) chicken flavor ramen noodle soup

1 Cook the chicken in a 10-inch nonstick skillet over medium-high heat until well browned, stirring often. Remove the chicken from the skillet.

2 Stir the mushroom soup, water, vegetables and **1** ramen seasoning packet in the skillet and heat to a boil. (Reserve the remaining seasoning packet for another use.) Reduce the heat to medium and cook for 5 minutes, stirring often.

3 Break up the noodles and stir in the skillet. Return the chicken to the skillet and cook for 5 minutes or until the chicken is cooked through and the noodles are tender, stirring occasionally.

Prep Time: 10 minutes
Cook Time: 20 minutes

100

Noodle Bowls

Ginger Beef & Noodle Bowls

Makes 4 servings

1   pound beef shoulder top blade (flat iron) steaks or
      1 beef top round steak, cut ¾ inch thick

1   tablespoon dark sesame oil

2   tablespoons minced fresh ginger

2   large cloves garlic, minced

     Salt and black pepper

2   cans (13¾ to 14½ ounces each) ready-to-serve beef broth

¾   cup thinly sliced green onions

2   tablespoons mirin or rice wine vinegar

6   cups cooked fresh Oriental-style thin cut noodles or unseasoned
      instant ramen noodles

½   cup shredded carrots

1 Cut steaks crosswise into ¼-inch thick strips; cut strips in half. Heat ½ tablespoon sesame oil in large nonstick skillet over medium-high heat until hot. Add ginger and garlic; cook 1 minute. Add ½ of beef; stir-fry 2 minutes or until outside surface of beef is no longer pink. Remove from skillet. Repeat with remaining oil and beef. Season with salt and pepper, as desired. Keep warm.

2 Add broth, green onions and mirin to skillet; bring to a boil. Reduce heat to low; simmer 8 to 10 minutes.

3 Meanwhile divide noodles and beef evenly among 4 large soup bowls.

4 Bring broth mixture to a boil over high heat; ladle boiling mixture evenly over beef and noodles. Garnish with carrots.

Favorite recipe courtesy **The Beef Checkoff**

Noodle Bowls

Italian Vegetable Soup with Noodles

Makes 6 servings

3	cups water
1½	cups **V8**® 100% Vegetable Juice
½	teaspoon dried oregano leaves, crushed
⅛	teaspoon ground black pepper
1	small zucchini, cut into cubes (about 1 cup)
1	package (3 ounces) chicken flavor ramen noodle soup
1	can (about 15 ounces) red **or** white kidney beans (cannellini), rinsed and drained

1 Stir the water, vegetable juice, oregano, pepper and zucchini in a 4-quart saucepan. Heat to a boil over medium-high heat.

2 Stir the noodles in the saucepan. Reduce the heat to medium. Cook for 5 minutes or until the zucchini is tender. Add the ramen seasoning packet and beans and heat through.

Prep Time: 10 minutes
Cook Time: 15 minutes

Noodle Bowls

Creamy Chicken Broccoli Noodles

2 packages (3 ounces each) chicken flavor ramen
   noodle soup

1 can (10¾ ounces) Campbell's® Condensed Cream of
   Mushroom Soup (Regular **or** 98% Fat Free)

½ can milk

1½ cups cooked broccoli florets

1½ cups cubed cooked chicken

6 cherry tomatoes, cut into quarters (optional)

1 Cook noodles in saucepan according to package directions. Stir in seasoning packets. Drain off most of liquid.

2 Add mushroom soup, milk, broccoli and chicken. Heat through. Stir in tomatoes.

Prep Time: 5 minutes
Cook Time: 20 minutes

Ramen Alfredo

Makes 3 servings

1	**cup whipping cream**
¼	**teaspoon salt**
¼	**teaspoon black pepper**
⅛	**teaspoon nutmeg**
3	**packages (3 ounces each) ramen noodles, any flavor***
½	**cup grated Parmesan cheese, plus additional for garnish**

*Discard seasoning packets.

1 Combine cream, salt, pepper and nutmeg in large saucepan; cook over medium heat 8 minutes or until reduced to ½ cup, stirring occasionally.

2 Bring large saucepan of water to a boil. Add noodles; cook 1 minute. Drain noodles, reserving ¼ cup cooking water.

3 Add reserved cooking water and ½ cup cheese to cream mixture; bring to a simmer over medium-high heat. Reduce heat to medium-low; add noodles, tossing to coat. Cook 1 minute or until noodles are al dente and cheese is melted. Sprinkle with additional cheese.

Tip: Make Chicken Alfredo by adding chopped cooked chicken to this dish.

Beefy Noodle Skillet

Makes 4 servings

2   packages (3 ounces **each**) beef flavor ramen
        noodle soup

¾   pound extra lean ground beef

1   medium onion, chopped (about ½ cup)

¼   teaspoon garlic powder

1   can (10¾ ounces) Campbell's® Condensed Tomato
        Soup

¼   cup water

1 Heat **4 cups** water in a 3-quart saucepan over medium-high heat to a boil. Break up the noodles and stir into the saucepan. Reduce the heat to medium. Cook for 3 minutes or until the noodles are tender. Drain the noodles well in a colander.

2 Cook the beef, onion and garlic powder in a 10-inch skillet over medium-high heat until the beef is well browned, stirring often to separate meat. Pour off any fat.

3 Stir the tomato soup, water, noodles and **1** ramen seasoning packet in the skillet. (Reserve remaining seasoning packet for another use.) Cook until the mixture is hot and bubbling, stirring occasionally.

Prep Time: 5 minutes
Cook Time: 25 minutes

Fast Food Faves

Chunky Chicken Stir-Fry

1   tablespoon vegetable oil

4   skinless, boneless chicken breast halves (about 1 pound), cut into strips

1   can (19 ounces) Campbell's® Chunky™ Savory Vegetable Soup

1   cup frozen stir-fry **or** other mixed vegetable combination, thawed

2   teaspoons soy sauce

2   teaspoons cornstarch

2   packages (3 ounces **each**) oriental flavor ramen noodle soup

1 Heat the oil in a 10-inch skillet over medium-high heat. Add the chicken and stir-fry until well browned. Remove the chicken from the skillet.

2 Stir the vegetable soup, vegetables, soy sauce and cornstarch in the skillet. Return the chicken to the skillet. Cook and stir until the mixture boils and thickens.

3 Prepare the ramen noodle soup according to the package directions. Drain off the liquid. Serve the chicken mixture over the noodles.

Tip: To thaw the frozen vegetables, microwave on HIGH for 2 minutes or until thawed.

Prep Time: 10 minutes
Cook Time: 20 minutes

Ramen Pepperoni & Cheese Casserole

Makes 6 to 8 servings

2	tablespoons unsalted butter, divided
1	cup panko bread crumbs
½	teaspoon plus ⅛ teaspoon salt, divided
4	packages (3 ounces each) ramen noodles, any flavor, broken into chunks*
30	pepperoni slices
1½	cups pasta sauce
1	tablespoon all-purpose flour
1½	cups milk
½	teaspoon dried Italian herbs
¼	teaspoon black pepper
2	cups shredded sharp Cheddar cheese, divided
1	cup shredded mozzarella cheese

Discard seasoning packets.

1 Preheat oven to 400°F. Grease 13×9-inch baking dish.

2 Melt 1 tablespoon butter in large skillet over medium heat. Add panko and ⅛ teaspoon salt; cook 6 minutes or until lightly toasted, stirring occasionally. Transfer to small bowl.

3 Cook noodles according to package directions. Drain and rinse with cold water. Transfer to large bowl.

4 Place pepperoni on microwavable plate; microwave on HIGH 1 minute. Blot grease with paper towels. Add half of the pepperoni and pasta sauce to noodles.

5 Melt remaining 1 tablespoon butter in skillet over medium heat. Add flour; cook 1 minute. Add milk, remaining ½ teaspoon salt, Italian herbs and pepper; cook and stir 4 minutes or until thickened. Remove from heat; stir in 1½ cups Cheddar cheese and mozzarella cheese until melted. Add to ramen mixture; stir until noodles are evenly coated. Transfer to prepared dish.

6 Sprinkle with remaining ½ cup Cheddar cheese, remaining pepperoni and panko. Bake 35 to 40 minutes or until bubbly and cheese is golden. Let stand 5 minutes before serving.

Shrimp Ramen Pad Thai

Makes 4 to 6 servings

7¼	cups water, divided
3	packages (3 ounces each) ramen noodles, any flavor*
4	tablespoons vegetable oil, divided
3	tablespoons packed light brown sugar
3	tablespoons soy sauce
2	tablespoons lime juice
1	tablespoon anchovy paste
2	eggs, lightly beaten
12	ounces medium shrimp, peeled and deveined
2	cloves garlic, minced
1	tablespoon paprika
¼	to ½ teaspoon ground red pepper
8	ounces fresh bean sprouts, divided
½	cup coarsely chopped unsalted dry-roasted peanuts
4	green onions with tops, cut into 1-inch lengths
½	lime, cut lengthwise into 4 wedges (optional)

Discard seasoning packets.

1 Place 6 cups water in wok; bring to a boil over high heat. Add noodles; cook 2 minutes or until tender but still firm, stirring frequently. Drain and rinse under cold running water to stop cooking. Drain again and place noodles in large bowl. Add 1 tablespoon oil; toss lightly to coat. Set aside.

2 Combine remaining 1¼ cups water, brown sugar, soy sauce, lime juice and anchovy paste in small bowl; set aside.

3 Heat wok over medium heat about 30 seconds or until hot. Drizzle 1 tablespoon oil into wok and heat 15 seconds. Add eggs and cook 1 minute or just until set on bottom. Turn eggs over and stir to scramble until cooked but not dry. Transfer to medium bowl; set aside.

4 Heat wok over high heat until hot. Drizzle 1 tablespoon oil into wok and heat 15 seconds. Add shrimp and garlic; stir-fry 2 minutes or until shrimp begin to turn pink and opaque. Add shrimp to eggs.

5 Heat wok over medium heat until hot. Drizzle remaining 1 tablespoon oil into wok and heat 15 seconds. Stir in paprika and red pepper. Add cooked noodles and anchovy mixture; cook and stir about 5 minutes or until noodles

Fast Food Fares

are softened. Stir in three-fourths of the bean sprouts. Add peanuts and green onions; toss and cook about 1 minute or until onions begin to wilt.

6 Add eggs and shrimp; stir-fry until heated through. Transfer to serving plate and garnish with remaining bean sprouts and lime wedges. Sprinkle with additional chopped peanuts, if desired.

Peanut Noodles

Makes 4 servings

- 3 tablespoons vegetable oil, divided
- 2 tablespoons peanut butter
- 1 tablespoon teriyaki sauce
-    Juice of 1 lime
- 1 teaspoon chili-garlic paste (optional)
- 2 packages (3 ounces each) ramen noodles, any flavor*
- ¾ cup shelled edamame, thawed if frozen
- ½ cup thinly sliced red bell pepper
-    Crushed peanuts (optional)

Discard seasoning packets.

1 Combine 2 tablespoons oil, peanut butter, teriyaki sauce, lime juice and chili-garlic paste, if desired, in large bowl.

2 Bring water to a boil in medium saucepan over medium-high heat. Add noodles and edamame; boil 2 minutes. Drain and rinse with cold water. Toss with remaining 1 tablespoon oil.

3 Combine noodle mixture and bell pepper with peanut butter mixture; toss to coat. Top with peanuts, if desired.

Fast Food Fares

Pad Thai

Makes 5 servings

8	ounces uncooked rice noodles, ⅛ inch thick*
2	tablespoons rice wine vinegar
1½	tablespoons fish sauce**
1	to 2 tablespoons fresh lemon juice
1	tablespoon ketchup
2	teaspoons sugar
¼	teaspoon red pepper flakes
1	tablespoon vegetable oil
1	boneless, skinless chicken breast (about 4 ounces), finely chopped
2	green onions, thinly sliced
2	cloves garlic, minced
3	ounces small raw shrimp, peeled
2	cups fresh bean sprouts
¾	cup shredded red cabbage
1	medium carrot, shredded
3	tablespoons minced fresh cilantro
2	tablespoons chopped unsalted dry-roasted peanuts
	Lime wedges

*Substitute 2 packages (3 ounces each) ramen noodles, any flavor, for the rice noodles.

**Fish sauce is available at most larger supermarkets and Asian markets.

1 Place noodles in medium bowl. Cover with lukewarm water; let stand 30 minutes or until soft. Drain and set aside. (If using ramen noodles, prepare according to package directions.) Combine rice wine vinegar, fish sauce, lemon juice, ketchup, sugar and red pepper flakes in small bowl.

2 Heat oil in wok or large nonstick skillet over medium-high heat. Add chicken, green onions and garlic. Cook and stir until chicken is no longer pink. Stir in noodles; cook 1 minute. Add shrimp; cook about 3 minutes, just until shrimp turn pink and opaque. Stir in fish sauce mixture; toss to coat evenly. Add bean sprouts and cook until heated through, about 2 minutes.

3 Serve with shredded cabbage, carrot, cilantro, peanuts and lime wedges.

Ramen "Spaghetti" Tacos

Makes 4 servings

2   packages (3 ounces each) ramen noodles, any flavor*

1   cup pasta sauce

8   hard taco shells

½   cup grated mozzarella cheese

¼   cup shredded Cheddar cheese

     Chopped tomatoes

*Discard seasoning packets.

1 Cook noodles according to package directions. Drain; return to saucepan. Add pasta sauce. Cook over medium heat until heated throughout.

2 Divide noodles evenly among taco shells. Top each taco with mozzarella and Cheddar cheeses. Microwave on HIGH at 10- to 15-second intervals until cheese is melted, if desired. Top with tomatoes.

Tip: These tacos can be flavored in a variety of ways. Try them with salsa instead of pasta sauce and toppings such as sour cream, guacamole, shredded lettuce and grated Mexican cheese. Or, mix cooked noodles with teriyaki sauce and top with shredded cabbage, water chestnuts, bamboo shoots and chicken or pork.

Skillet "Spaghetti" Toss

Makes 3 to 4 servings

2   tablespoons olive oil

1   cup sliced mushrooms

1   cup broccoli florets

2   Italian chicken sausages, sliced

2   packages (3 ounces each) ramen noodles, any flavor, broken in half*

1   to 1½ cups pasta sauce

   Grated Parmesan cheese

Discard seasoning packets.

1 Heat oil in large skillet over medium-high heat. Add mushrooms, broccoli and sausage; cook and stir 10 minutes or until broccoli is crisp-tender.

2 Meanwhile, bring water to a boil in medium saucepan. Boil noodles 2 minutes; drain well.

3 Add pasta sauce and noodles to skillet; toss to coat. Reduce heat to medium; cook until heated through. Top with cheese.

Presto Pesto

Makes 1 serving

1 package (3 ounces) ramen noodles, any flavor, broken in half*

1 tablespoon prepared pesto sauce

2 teaspoons pine nuts, toasted

5 grape tomatoes, halved

Salt

Discard seasoning packet.

1 Cook noodles according to package directions; drain well.

2 Combine noodles and pesto sauce in medium bowl. Add pine nuts, tomatoes and salt; toss to coat.

Tip: This easy-to-make dish can also become a quick entrée. Cut up and brown 1 skinless, boneless chicken breast and toss in with the ingredients.

Shanghai Noodles

Makes 6 servings

- 6 ounces uncooked ramen noodles or angel hair pasta
- 1 package (16 ounces) JOHNSONVILLE® Stadium Style Brats or Smoked Brats, coin-sliced
- 1 package (16 ounces) frozen stir-fry vegetable blend
- 1 tablespoon water
- ¼ cup stir-fry sauce
- 2 tablespoons apricot jam
- 1 teaspoon sesame oil (optional)
- 1 tablespoon sesame seeds, toasted

Prepare noodles according to package directions; drain (discard seasoning packet). Meanwhile, in large skillet or wok, combine the coin-sliced brats, vegetables and water. Cover and cook over medium-high heat for 5 to 8 minutes or until hot. Combine the stir-fry sauce, jam and sesame oil; add to vegetable mixture. Stir-fry for 2 to 3 minutes or until vegetables are crisp-tender. Serve over noodles; sprinkle with sesame seeds.

Quick & Easy Chicken Pesto Salad

Makes 2 servings

1 package (3 ounces) ramen noodles, any flavor, broken into 4 large chunks*

1 cup chopped cooked chicken

½ cup halved grape tomatoes

¼ cup slivered or finely chopped carrots

1 to 2 tablespoons prepared pesto

Salt and black pepper

Discard seasoning packet.

1 Bring water to a boil in medium saucepan. Boil noodles 2 minutes. Drain and rinse with cold water.

2 Combine noodles, chicken, tomatoes, carrots and pesto in large bowl; toss to coat. Season with salt and pepper.

Crunchy Salmon Patties

Makes 8 patties

1 package (3 ounces) oriental-flavored ramen noodles

¼ cup all-purpose flour

2 cans (6 ounces each) pink salmon, drained and flaked

¼ cup finely diced onion

¼ cup finely diced red bell pepper

2 eggs, lightly beaten

2 tablespoons vegetable oil

1 Place noodles, flour and seasoning packet in food processor; process until noodles become finely chopped.

2 Place salmon, onion, bell pepper and half of noodle mixture in large bowl; mix well. Add eggs; stir to combine.

3 Place remaining noodle mixture on plate. Form salmon mixture into 8 patties. Press both sides of patties into noodle mixture.

4 Heat oil in large skillet over medium-high heat. Cook patties in batches 3 to 5 minutes per side or until golden brown.

Note: Try these patties with tartar sauce, sweet and sour sauce or Asian spicy mustard.

Ramen Pizza Pie

Makes 6 servings

  2   **packages (3 ounces each) ramen noodles, any flavor***

  2   **eggs, lightly beaten**

¼   **cup milk**

¼   **teaspoon salt**

  1   **cup ricotta cheese**

  1   **cup pasta sauce****

  1   **cup (4 ounces) shredded part-skim mozzarella cheese**

*Discard seasoning packets.

**For added flavor, choose a tomato-basil flavored sauce.

1 Preheat oven to 425°F. Grease a 9-inch pie pan. Cook and drain noodles according to package directions.

2 Whisk eggs, milk and salt in large bowl. Stir in noodles; toss to coat. Spread evenly in bottom of prepared pan. Bake 10 minutes or until set.

3 Top crust with ricotta, pasta sauce and mozzarella cheese. Bake 15 minutes or until cheese is melted and golden brown. Let stand 5 minutes before serving.

Fast Food Fares

Tuna Ramen Casserole

Makes 2 to 3 servings

2	packages (3 ounces each) ramen noodles, any flavor, broken in half*
¾	cup broccoli florets
1	can (about 5 ounces) tuna in water, drained and flaked
¾	cup (3 ounces) shredded Italian cheese blend, divided
½	cup milk
¼	cup mayonnaise
1	teaspoon salt
¼	teaspoon red pepper flakes

Discard seasoning packets.

1 Preheat oven to 350°F. Grease 8-inch glass baking dish.

2 Bring water to a boil in medium saucepan over medium heat. Boil noodles 1 minute. Add broccoli florets. Boil noodles and broccoli 1 minute more. Drain and rinse with cold water.

3 Combine tuna, ½ cup cheese, milk, mayonnaise, salt and red pepper flakes in large bowl. Stir in noodles and broccoli. Spread in prepared dish. Top with remaining ¼ cup cheese.

4 Bake 15 minutes or until cheese is melted.

Tip: Adding broccoli and cheese to your tuna casserole makes this an all-in-one meal.

Fast Food Fares

Chinese Chicken Salad Sandwiches

¼ **cup soy sauce**

¼ **cup rice wine vinegar**

¼ **cup vegetable or peanut oil**

¼ **cup roasted sesame seed oil**

2 **tablespoons fresh ginger, minced**

4 **teaspoons sugar**

4 **teaspoons dry mustard**

2 **pounds chicken breast, boned, skinned, steamed and cubed**

1 **large red onion (about 9 to 11 ounces), cut into narrow wedges**

1 **cup pea pods, fresh or thawed frozen, slivered**

6 **crusty round rolls, split, buttered**

   Lettuce or watercress

4 **teaspoons sesame seeds, toasted**

   Crispy noodles (optional)

Mix dressing of soy sauce, vinegar, oils, ginger, sugar and mustard. Add chicken, onions and pea pods. Toss well. Chill at least 4 hours to blend flavors. Fill each roll with lettuce and chicken salad. Sprinkle with sesame seeds. Serve with crispy noodles, if desired.

Favorite recipe from **National Onion Association**

Chicken & Vegetable Lo Mein

Makes 4 servings

1¼ pounds skinless, boneless chicken breasts, cut into cubes

1 can (10¾ ounces) Campbell's® Condensed Cream of Mushroom Soup (Regular **or** 98% Fat Free)

1¾ cups water

2 cups frozen vegetable combination (broccoli, cauliflower, carrots)

2 packages (2.8 ounces **each**) oriental flavor ramen noodle soup

1 Cook the chicken in a 10-inch nonstick skillet over medium-high heat until well browned, stirring often. Remove the chicken from the skillet.

2 Stir the mushroom soup, water, vegetables and **1** ramen seasoning packet in the skillet and heat to a boil. (Reserve the remaining seasoning packet for another use.) Reduce the heat to medium and cook for 5 minutes, stirring often.

3 Break up the noodles and stir in the skillet. Return the chicken to the skillet and cook for 5 minutes or until the chicken is cooked through and the noodles are tender, stirring occasionally.

Prep Time: 10 minutes
Cook Time: 20 minutes

Fast Food Fares

Tomato Chicken Stir-Fry with Noodles

Makes 4 servings

Vegetable cooking spray

3 cups cut-up fresh vegetables (broccoli florets, carrots cut into matchstick-thin strips **and** green **or** red pepper strips)

¼ teaspoon garlic powder **or** 2 small cloves garlic, minced

4 skinless, boneless chicken breasts halves (about 1 pound), cut into very thin strips

1 can (10¾ ounces) Campbell's® Healthy Request® Condensed Tomato Soup

1 tablespoon vinegar

2 teaspoons low-sodium soy sauce

⅛ teaspoon hot pepper sauce

2 packages (3 ounces **each**) chicken flavor ramen noodle soup

1 Spray a 10-inch skillet with the cooking spray and heat over medium-high heat for 1 minute. Add the vegetables and garlic powder and stir-fry until the vegetables are tender-crisp. Remove the vegetables from the skillet. Remove the skillet from the heat.

2 Spray the skillet with the cooking spray and heat over medium-high heat for 1 minute. Add the chicken and stir-fry until well browned. Remove the chicken from the skillet.

3 Stir the soup, vinegar, soy sauce and hot pepper sauce in the skillet and heat to a boil. Reduce the heat to low. Return the vegetables and chicken to the skillet. Cook until the mixture is hot and bubbling, stirring occasionally.

4 Cook the noodles according to the package directions without the seasoning packets. (Reserve the seasoning packets for another use.) Drain the noodles well in a colander. Serve the chicken mixture over the noodles.

Prep Time: 15 minutes
Cook Time: 25 minutes

Crunchy Munchies

Glazed Noodle Crunch

¼   **cup (½ stick) butter, cut into small pieces**

½   **cup packed light brown sugar**

½   **teaspoon cinnamon**

1   **package (3 ounces) ramen noodles, any flavor, broken into bite-size pieces***

1   **cup pretzels, broken into pieces**

1   **cup salted peanuts**

½   **cup dried cranberries**

*Discard seasoning packet.

Melt butter in medium microwavable bowl on HIGH 30 seconds. Stir in brown sugar and cinnamon; microwave 1½ minutes, stirring after first minute. Stir in noodles. Spread mixture on waxed paper; cool completely. Place in large bowl; toss with pretzels, peanuts and cranberries.

Tip: Add ½ cup semisweet chocolate chips to the mixture for additional color and sweetness.

Open-Faced "S'Mores"

Makes 4 s'mores

1   package (3 ounces) ramen noodles, any flavor*

2   chocolate bars (1.5 ounces each), broken into sections

4   large marshmallows, halved

Discard seasoning packet.

1 Cut noodles in half horizontally with serrated knife, to make 2 squares. Cut each square in half crosswise, making 4 rectangles in total.

2 Divide chocolate pieces evenly over each rectangle. Heat in microwave on HIGH 10 seconds. Continue to microwave at 10-second intervals until chocolate just begins to melt.

3 Top each noodle rectangle with 2 halves of marshmallows. Return to microwave 15 seconds or until marshmallows are puffed.

Note: The marshmallows can be toasted on a skewer over medium-high flame on the stovetop, if desired. You can also substitute hazelnut chocolate spread for the chocolate bars; if so omit step 2.

Crunchy Munchies

Chocolate Ramen Fudge

Makes 18 servings

1   package (12 ounces) semisweet chocolate chips

1   can (14 ounces) sweetened condensed milk

1   package (3 ounces) ramen noodles, any flavor, broken into bite-size pieces*

2   tablespoons butter, softened

1   teaspoon vanilla

Discard seasoning packet.

1 Line 8-inch square baking pan with foil, extending foil over edges of pan.

2 Place chocolate chips in medium microwavable bowl. Microwave on HIGH 1 minute; stir. Repeat, if necessary for 30-second intervals, stirring after each, until completely melted. Mix in sweetened condensed milk, noodles, butter and vanilla.

3 Transfer mixture into prepared pan; spread evenly. Refrigerate 1 hour or until firm. Remove from pan; peel off foil. Cut into squares.

Crunchy Munchies

Salad Crunchies

Makes 1 (1-pint) jar

1	package (3 ounces) ramen noodles, any flavor*
⅓	cup sesame seeds (about 1½ ounces)
¾	cup roasted, unsalted cashew pieces (about 4 ounces)

Discard seasoning packet.

1 Preheat oven to 350°F. Line baking sheet with foil. Set aside.

2 Break noodles into pieces onto prepared baking sheet. Spread out in single layer. Sprinkle sesame seeds evenly over noodle pieces.

3 Bake 4 to 6 minutes or until sesame seeds are golden and fragrant, stirring once. Remove baking sheet from oven. Cool noodle mixture.

4 Combine noodle mixture and cashew pieces in mixing bowl. Transfer mixture to 1-pint wide-mouth jar. Seal jar.

5 Decorate jar and attach gift tag/recipe card.

Tip: Sprinkle on any salad for a crunchy, nutty flavor topping. It is also great as a snack.

Quick Oriental Chicken Salad: Purchase a roasted chicken, a bag of salad greens, a can of mandarin oranges, green onions and a bottle of oriental salad dressing. Combine bag of salad greens with ½ to 1 cup shredded chicken. Add drained mandarin oranges and sliced green onions. Toss with dressing and top with Salad Crunchies.

Rocky Road Bundles

Makes 1 dozen treats

1   **cup semisweet chocolate chips**

½   **cup creamy peanut butter**

1   **package (3 ounces) ramen noodles, any flavor, broken into bite-size pieces***

1   **cup mini marshmallows**

*Discard seasoning packet.

1 Combine chocolate chips and peanut butter in microwavable bowl. Microwave on MEDIUM (50%) 1 minute; stir. Repeat if necessary, stirring after 15-second intervals, until chocolate is melted and mixture is well blended.

2 Add noodles and marshmallows; mix well. Drop by tablespoonfuls onto baking sheet lined with waxed paper; refrigerate 1 hour or until firm.

Tip: These easy, no-bake bundles make a great treat for parties, gatherings and family-time fun.

Index

Index

Index

Acknowledgments

The publisher would like to thank the companies and organizations listed below
for the use of their recipes and photos in this publication.

The Beef Checkoff
Campbell Soup Company
Dole Food Company, Inc.
Fisher® Nuts
®Johnsonville Sausage, LLC
National Onion Association

National Sunflower Association
Nestlé USA
North Dakota Beef Commission
Reckitt Benckiser LLC
StarKist®
TexaSweet Citrus Marketing, Inc.

Index

METRIC CONVERSION CHART

VOLUME MEASUREMENTS (dry)

1/8 teaspoon = 0.5 mL
1/4 teaspoon = 1 mL
1/2 teaspoon = 2 mL
3/4 teaspoon = 4 mL
1 teaspoon = 5 mL
1 tablespoon = 15 mL
2 tablespoons = 30 mL
1/4 cup = 60 mL
1/3 cup = 75 mL
1/2 cup = 125 mL
2/3 cup = 150 mL
3/4 cup = 175 mL
1 cup = 250 mL
2 cups = 1 pint = 500 mL
3 cups = 750 mL
4 cups = 1 quart = 1 L

VOLUME MEASUREMENTS (fluid)

1 fluid ounce (2 tablespoons) = 30 mL
4 fluid ounces (1/2 cup) = 125 mL
8 fluid ounces (1 cup) = 250 mL
12 fluid ounces (1 1/2 cups) = 375 mL
16 fluid ounces (2 cups) = 500 mL

WEIGHTS (mass)

1/2 ounce = 15 g
1 ounce = 30 g
3 ounces = 90 g
4 ounces = 120 g
8 ounces = 225 g
10 ounces = 285 g
12 ounces = 360 g
16 ounces = 1 pound = 450 g

DIMENSIONS

1/16 inch = 2 mm
1/8 inch = 3 mm
1/4 inch = 6 mm
1/2 inch = 1.5 cm
3/4 inch = 2 cm
1 inch = 2.5 cm

OVEN TEMPERATURES

250°F = 120°C
275°F = 140°C
300°F = 150°C
325°F = 160°C
350°F = 180°C
375°F = 190°C
400°F = 200°C
425°F = 220°C
450°F = 230°C

BAKING PAN SIZES

Utensil	Size in Inches/Quarts	Metric Volume	Size in Centimeters
Baking or Cake Pan (square or rectangular)	8×8×2	2 L	20×20×5
	9×9×2	2.5 L	23×23×5
	12×8×2	3 L	30×20×5
	13×9×2	3.5 L	33×23×5
Loaf Pan	8×4×3	1.5 L	20×10×7
	9×5×3	2 L	23×13×7
Round Layer Cake Pan	8×1½	1.2 L	20×4
	9×1½	1.5 L	23×4
Pie Plate	8×1¼	750 mL	20×3
	9×1¼	1 L	23×3
Baking Dish or Casserole	1 quart	1 L	—
	1½ quarts	1.5 L	—
	2 quarts	2 L	—